THE IMPACT OF ENVIRONMENTALISM: CONSERVATION

Jen Green

www.raintreepublishers.co.uk
Visit our website to find out
more information about
Raintree books.

To order:
☎ Phone 0845 6044371
🖹 Fax +44 (0) 1865 312263
🖂 Email myorders@raintreepublishers.co.uk

Customers from outside the UK please telephone +44 1865 312262

Raintree is an imprint of Capstone Global Library
Limited, a company incorporated in England and
Wales having its registered office at 7 Pilgrim Street,
London, EC4V 6LB – Registered company number:
6695582

Edited by Andrew Farrow, Adam Miller, and
    Diyan Leake
Designed by Victoria Allen
Picture research by Elizabeth Alexander
Illustrations by Oxford Designers & Illustrators
Originated by Capstone Global Library Ltd
Printed and bound in China by Leo Paper Products Ltd

ISBN 978 1 406 23858 7
16 15 14 13 12
10 9 8 7 6 5 4 3 2 1

British Library Cataloguing in Publication Data
A full catalogue record for this book is available from
the British Library.

Acknowledgements
The author and publisher are grateful to the following
for permission to reproduce copyright material:
Alamy pp. 36 (© John Warburton-Lee Photography/
Nigel Pavitt), 51 (© Alaskastock/Kenneth R. Whitten);
Getty Images pp. 13 (Ulet Ifansasti), 19 (Joe Raedle),
21 (AFP/Jeremy Sutton-Hibbert), 35 (Paul Souders),
41 (ColorChinaPhoto/He Dalu), 45 (James Ambler/
Barcroft USA); www.msc.org p. 48; Nature Picture
Library p. 54 (© Ingo Arndt); Photolibrary pp. 7 (Harpe
Harpe), 15 (epa/Laszlo Czika), 29 (Britain on View/
Richard Watson), 33 (Top Photo Corporation), 38
(OSF/David Haring/DUPC); Press Association Images
pp. 9 (Scanpix/Rolf M. Aagaard), 25 (AAP Image/
Dean Lewins); Shutterstock pp. 11 (© Lee Prince), 16
(© Brandelet), 23 (© guentermanaus), 27 (© Susan
Flashman), 31 (© magutosh), 43 (© Wunson), 46
(© Anan Kaewkhammul), 52 (© Yvonne Pijnenburg-
Schonewille), 57 (© gary718); SuperStock p. 49
(© Cultura Limited).

Cover photograph of (top) a pile of tusks, reproduced
with permission of Shutterstock (© Joe Mercier),
and (bottom) a herd of elephants, reproduced with
permission of Shutterstock (© Johan Swanepoel).

Every effort has been made to contact copyright
holders of material reproduced in this book. Any
omissions will be rectified in subsequent printings if
notice is given to the publisher.

Disclaimer
All the internet addresses (URLs) given in this book
were valid at the time of going to press. However, due
to the dynamic nature of the internet, some addresses
may have changed, or sites may have changed or
ceased to exist since publication. While the author and
publisher regret any inconvenience this may cause
readers, no responsibility for any such changes can be
accepted by either the author or the publisher.

CONTENTS

What is conservation? 4

What is environmentalism? 6

Why conserve nature? 10

Why conserve wildlife? 18

Nature conservation 28

Wildlife conservation 40

What is the future of conservation?.......50

What have we learned? 56

Timeline...58

Glossary 60

Find out more 62

Index 64

Words printed in **bold** are explained in the Glossary.

WHAT IS CONSERVATION?

Did you know that an estimated 40 per cent of all species are threatened with **extinction** because of humans? That includes one-quarter of all mammal species and 12 per cent of birds. These facts are alarming but true, according to the **International Union for Conservation of Nature (IUCN)**, an organization that monitors **biodiversity** worldwide. Of course, extinctions have always happened naturally, but IUCN scientists believe that extinction is now happening at between 1,000 and 10,000 times the natural rate.

According to one estimate, 18,000 species are dying out each year – that's one species every half-hour. In 1992, 150 nations signed a key agreement to maintain Earth's biodiversity. This agreement was called the Convention on Biological Diversity. It concluded that: "We are creating the greatest extinction crisis since the natural disaster that wiped out the dinosaurs 65 million years ago".

Earth's biodiversity has been shaped through the process of evolution ever since life began 3.8 billion years ago. Over this period, there have been several major events when many species died out at once. Now, however, scientists have discovered Earth's biodiversity is again being threatened with a great extinction, this one caused by human activities. On every part of the planet, people are now affecting living **ecosystems**, as we alter **habitats** and produce pollution.

Any answers?

What can be done about this new wave of extinctions? That's where environmentalism comes in. For over a century, environmentalists have warned of the harmful effects of pollution. Environmental groups have worked to save rare species and habitats such as rainforests. Now most people understand the importance of **conservation**, and many people do something about it.

Environmentalists believe that governments and industry have a major role to play in conservation. But it is also down to each and every one of us to do our bit, because the everyday actions we take add up to affect the whole planet. Environmentalists believe that the energy we use, the waste we produce, and the choices we make as shoppers, impact on distant habitats and affect wildlife as diverse as coral reefs and polar bears. The Convention on Biological Diversity sums it up: "It is the choices and actions of billions of individuals that will determine whether or not biodiversity is conserved".

Preserving biodiversity

Conservation is action taken to protect the natural world and wildlife. The aim of conservation is to protect biodiversity – the variety of living things on Earth. To date, scientists have identified about 1.2 million living species, of an estimated total of 8.7 million species. Earth's biodiversity is sustained by habitats such as forests and grasslands. The living things in a habitat are interconnected in a web of life, forming living ecosystems that are studied by scientists called **ecologists**.

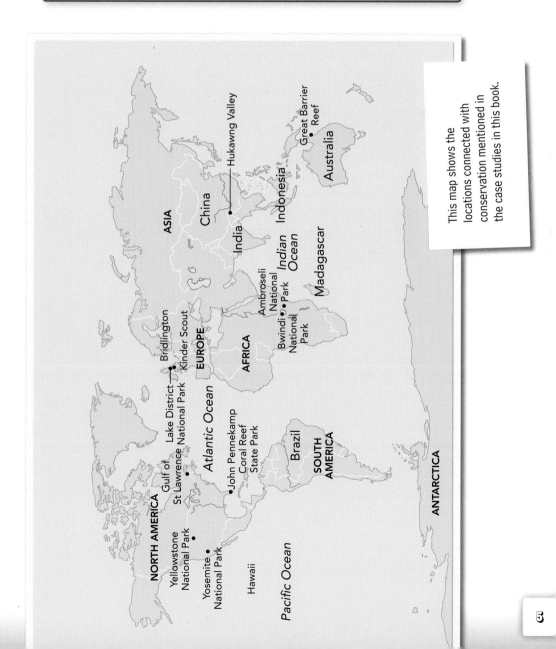

This map shows the locations connected with conservation mentioned in the case studies in this book.

WHAT IS ENVIRONMENTALISM?

Environmentalism is the movement to protect the natural world from human activities that could harm it – for example, through pollution or **deforestation**. Environmentalists seek to protect all aspects of the living world, including the land, air, and oceans.

The environmental, or "green", movement includes groups of different sizes, from international and national organizations to small groups and individuals. Some groups campaign to publicize environmental issues and end harmful practices. They may **lobby** governments to pass laws to protect nature. Some "greens" actually enter politics to ensure that environmental issues are a government priority. The 1970s and 1980s saw the rise of green political parties in many countries, including Germany, Australia, and New Zealand. Other greens believe that it is more important to live a life in harmony with nature than to be active in the environmental movement.

The rise of environmentalism

As a movement, environmentalism began in the late 19th century, when naturalists and thinkers in North America and Europe campaigned to protect wild places from being spoiled by development. The work of activists such as US naturalist John Muir led to the creation of the first national parks and reserves.

Green hero: John Muir

Scottish-born US naturalist John Muir (1838–1914) was one of the first to call for the preservation of wild places. He was also among the first to realize the interdependence of living things. He wrote: "When one tugs at a single thing in nature, he finds it attached to the rest of the world". Muir's love of nature inspired millions of Americans, including US presidents. He helped to set up the first US national parks and founded the Sierra Club, America's first active environmental organization.

In the early 1900s, environmentalists in Europe and North America lobbied for action on pollution control and wildlife protection. Many governments passed laws to improve the quality of the air, water, and soil.

The mid-20th century saw the birth of international conservation following the creation of the United Nations (UN) in 1945. The International Union for Conservation of Nature (IUCN) was formed in 1948. In 1961, the IUCN helped to set up the World Wildlife Fund (WWF).

In 1972, an important conference called the UN Conference on the Human Environment led to a series of new laws and international agreements on environmental protection. In the 1980s, pressure groups such as Greenpeace, Earth First!, and the Rainforest Action Network made headlines through their campaigns to protect **endangered** wildlife and threatened habitats.

The 1980s saw the birth of the idea of **sustainable** development – managing natural resources to meet present human needs while conserving nature. In 1987, the UN published a groundbreaking report on sustainable development, called *Our Common Future*. Previously, ideas of progress were mainly about improved **infrastructure**, such as schools, roads, and economies. However, issues such as climate change (see pages 14–15) and the need to reduce waste through recycling came to the fore in the 1990s and early 2000s.

Conservation can involve all sorts of work with wildlife. Here, staff from a national park in Africa have tranquillized an elephant prior to moving it to another location.

Why protect the environment?

Before the 1850s, very few people thought there was a need for conservation. In newly industrialized regions, such as Europe and North America, the natural world was seen as unruly, frightening, and even evil – a force that was hostile to humankind, and therefore to be tamed and conquered. In those regions, the right of humans to exploit nature's riches was supported by the Bible, which taught that in the beginning, God gave man "dominion over every living thing".

In the early 1800s, white settlers moving west across America believed that natural resources, such as timber, minerals, bison, and beaver, were limitless and there for the taking. However, from the late 19th century, thinkers such as John Muir realized that nature could be exhausted, and species could become extinct. Muir and others came to believe that man's domination of the natural world through science and technology brought with it a responsibility to take care of nature.

Two strands of thought

By the early 1900s, two strands of environmentalism had developed in the United States. John Muir and the writer Henry David Thoreau were "protectionists" who believed that nature should be protected for its own sake. Conservationists such as Gifford Pinchot, head of the US Forestry Service, thought that natural resources should be conserved for future human use.

Deep ecology

These two key strands can still be seen in the environmental movement today. In the 1970s, Norwegian philosopher Arne Naess (see opposite) founded a radical form of environmentalism called **deep ecology**. This maintains the worth of all living things for their own sake, not because they are useful to humans. Supporters of deep ecology believe that plant and animal species have as much right to survive and flourish as humans. The movement also stresses the interdependence of all living things on Earth.

Related to this is a strand of environmentalism that maintains that conservation is vital because human survival depends on it. Many conservation groups have a human-centred approach to environmental protection. They maintain that we need to protect the environment or we will run out of things we need, such as timber, fish, clean air, and water. Groups that work for sustainability may be part of this strand.

Added to the list of resources such as timber, land, and minerals are new uses of nature, such as to provide medicines and increase scientific knowledge. New environmental sciences like ecology have enriched our understanding of the complexity of nature, and are now taught in schools and colleges.

"Wilderness has a right to exist for its own sake, and for the sake of the diversity of the life forms it shelters."

David Foreman
Founder of Earth First!

Green hero: *Arne Naess*

Arne Naess (1912–2009) was a Norwegian mountaineer and philosopher. He was the youngest person to become a full professor at the University of Oslo. In 1970, Naess and 300 campaigners chained themselves to rocks by a rugged waterfall in Norway to protest against plans to build a dam. Police broke up the protest and the dam was eventually built, but the experience led Naess to develop the theory of deep ecology.

WHY CONSERVE NATURE?

Since the dawn of farming around 11,000 years ago, and particularly in the last 300 years since the Industrial Revolution, people have brought changes to habitats worldwide. Ecologists define habitats as places that support particular communities of living things. They also divide Earth's surface into large habitats called **biomes**, such as tropical rainforests. Habitats can also be as small as a patch of waste ground in a city.

Habitat loss

Between 1960 and 2000, Earth's human population doubled, from 3 to 6 billion. By 2011, there were 7 billion people, and experts estimate we will be 9 billion by 2040. As humans have spread to every part of the planet, so we have destroyed or altered ecosystems. Grasslands have been ploughed up to create farmlands to grow food. Forests and marshlands have been cleared to make way for new settlements, and the roads, car parks, and airports that go with them. Rivers have been dammed to generate energy, and wild habitats have been torn up for mining and industry. All these changes result in habitat loss that puts wildlife at risk. Environmentalists regard habitat loss as the single biggest threat to biodiversity on land and in the oceans.

The national park movement

In the late 19th century, environmentalists decided that the best way to protect ecosystems and wildlife was to set aside untouched land as national parks and reserves. In 1872, Yellowstone National Park in the United States became the world's first national park. In the late 1880s, Australia, Canada, and New Zealand followed the US lead, and in the early 1900s, national parks were set up in Sweden, South Africa, and other countries. Since the 1950s, the park movement has accelerated. According to the IUCN, there were over 30,000 protected areas worldwide by 2000, totalling 13 million square kilometres (5 million square miles).

Most parks and reserves have strict rules about conservation. Plants and animals are protected by law, mining and industry are often banned, and development is kept to a minimum. Some 140 years after Yellowstone was set up, preserving whole ecosystems is still seen as the best way of conserving wildlife. However, as we will see, parks and reserves can be unpopular with local people, who may believe conservation makes it hard for them to earn a living. Governments and park authorities have to work hard to balance the needs of conservation with those of local communities.

Yellowstone National Park covers 8,983 square kilometres (3,468 square miles). It includes mountains, lakes, and volcanic features such as geysers and hot springs.

Then and Now
Yellowstone National Park

In the 1860s, US conservationists lobbied for the world's first national park to be created to protect the scenery around Yellowstone in the Rocky Mountains. The idea attracted considerable opposition from local people on the grounds that it would harm logging, mining, and hunting in the area. However, some regional businesses, notably the Northern Pacific Railroad, supported the scheme because they believed it would generate income from tourism. In 1872, the park was duly signed into law as a "public park or pleasuring ground for the benefit and enjoyment of the people". It now receives over 3 million visitors every year.

ENVIRONMENTALISM IN ACTION

Protecting the rainforests

Tropical rainforests cover just five per cent of Earth's surface, but support roughly one half of all plant and animal species on land. Yet these rich habitats are fast disappearing. Five hundred years ago, rainforests covered 15–18 million square kilometres (5–7 million square miles) worldwide; today there are just 6 million square kilometres (2 million square miles).

Every year, around 200,000 square kilometres (77,000 square miles) of forest is destroyed or **degraded** worldwide. Ancient forests in the Amazon and south-east Asia are being felled very rapidly, and often illegally, for their valuable hardwood timber. They are cleared to make way for new settlements, roads, mines, and hydroelectric schemes. Huge tracts of forest are cleared to ranch beef cattle, or to create oil palm plantations or soybean farms. It is obvious that if deforestation continues at the present rate, there may be no rainforests left within your lifetime.

Value of rainforests

The biodiversity of rainforests is incredibly valuable, both for its own sake and for humans. Hundreds of fruits, nuts, and vegetables were originally found in rainforests. Forest plants provide one-quarter of all medicines. In terms of the environment, forest trees not only anchor the soil but also release oxygen and absorb carbon dioxide. In addition, forest trees soak up moisture and release it slowly, regulating rainfall.

Save the forests

Over 50 years ago, environmentalists realized that deforestation was having a serious impact on rainforests worldwide. Groups such as WWF called for a ban on logging in ancient forests, which contain the greatest biodiversity.

Since the 1970s and 1980s, campaign groups such as Greenpeace and the Rainforest Action Network (RAN) have campaigned against the multinational companies based in the West that have been involved in deforestation. For example, fast-food chains are accused of importing beef from deforested land. Groups such as RAN have persuaded people to boycott the companies concerned, forcing the multinationals to back down.

In 2006, direct action by Greenpeace activists, and other groups, succeeded in winning the support of the fast-food chain McDonalds, and food retailers such as Marks and Spencer and Waitrose, in a campaign to ban the import of soy grown on deforested land.

As with any habitat, the establishment of protected areas is a major tool for conservation. For decades, groups such as WWF have worked to set up parks and reserves, in partnership with local governments and rainforest peoples. Huge funds are needed to establish the reserves and make sure they are properly managed and policed to prevent illegal logging. Over the last 20 or so years, some major successes have been achieved. Tumucumaque National Park in Brazil, set up in 2002, is larger than Belgium. In 2008, a new 4,000-square-kilometre (1,500-square-mile) park was established in Guyana. However, environmentalists say only 8 per cent of ancient forests worldwide are strictly protected, and illegal logging remains a problem.

An aerial view of stacked timber in a huge logging operation in Indonesia. Some forests are so remote that their destruction can only be monitored by satellite.

Pollution and its causes

Since the Industrial Revolution of the 18th and 19th centuries, and particularly in the last century, pollution has become a major threat to habitats and wildlife. Pollution is waste that is not properly disposed of, and ends up in the environment.

Mining and manufacturing, energy production, farming, cars, and household waste are all major sources of pollution. For example, waste gases from factories, cars, and power stations cause air pollution. Sewage from cities and fertilizers from farms spill into rivers, harming aquatic life. The oceans are polluted by waste dumped deliberately, and also by accidents such as oil spills. Soil and groundwater are polluted by waste from mining and rubbish dumped in landfills.

Pollution spreads quickly through air and water, dispersed by winds and ocean currents. It also spreads via food chains, where it is usually absorbed by microscopic life forms at the bottom of the chain. These are eaten by larger creatures, and the toxins pass up the chain and build up in top predators, such as seals, dolphins, and polar bears, that eat the poisoned prey. Traces of pollution are found in ecosystems worldwide, even in very remote places, and in all living things, including humans.

Global warming

In the 1980s, it became widely accepted by environmental scientists that carbon dioxide and other waste gases from factories, cars, and power stations were trapping more of the Sun's heat in the atmosphere, causing **global warming**. At first, some governments were reluctant to accept that global warming was caused by human activities, but by around 2000, the evidence was overwhelming. In the 20th century, global temperatures rose by 0.6–0.9°C (1.1–1.6°F). That might not sound like much, but one result was that sea levels rose by 20 centimetres (8 inches). Scientists believe temperatures may rise by 1.1–6.4°C (2–11°F) by 2100, depending on the amount of **emissions**. As that happens, the resulting climate change will have many potential effects, including threatening the survival of many species worldwide, as well as settlements on coasts.

Reducing pollution

The harmful effects of pollution have been recognized for over a century. Since the early 1990s, environmentalists have lobbied governments to pass anti-pollution laws. In the 1960s and 1970s, this resulted in pioneering legislation, such as Clean Air and Clean Water acts. Government agencies such as the US Environmental Protection Agency were set up to monitor pollution. In the 1990s, the problem of waste disposal was reduced thanks to environmental groups convincing governments, businesses, and ordinary people to recycle waste.

In the 1970s and 1980s, pressure groups such as Greenpeace publicized the dumping of waste in rivers and oceans. Partly thanks to public pressure, many countries signed international agreements to reduce pollution – for example, the Law of the Sea Treaty and the Ramsar Convention, which protects wetlands. However, population growth and rapid industrialization in countries such as China, India, and Brazil mean pollution remains a major threat to wildlife. They also make living things more vulnerable to disease.

In 2008, Greenpeace activists staged a protest at the Raba River in Australia, to publicize pollution that a local leather factory had produced.

ENVIRONMENTALISM IN ACTION

Protecting coral reefs

Coral reefs cover just a tiny fraction of the oceans, but are home to around one-third of all marine species. The richest reefs are found in shallow seas in the tropics because the anemone-like **polyps** that build the reefs flourish in warm water that is less than 50 metres (165 feet) deep. As well as having great ecological importance, coral reefs also generate huge amounts of income through tourism.

Threats to reefs

The world's coral reefs are under threat. Some marine biologists estimate that 10 per cent of reefs worldwide have been destroyed in the last 50 years, and another third could die by 2050. The IUCN puts the figure considerably higher, up to 70 per cent. Threats to coral reefs include overfishing, which can upset the balance of reef food chains. Tourism can also cause problems, including habitat loss when reefs are torn up to build new resorts, airports, and marinas. Boat anchors, swimmers, and divers can also damage delicate reefs.

Divers photograph angelfish on Australia's Great Barrier Reef, which is made up of 2,500 separate reefs.

The greatest threats to coral reefs come from pollution. The coral-building polyps and the algae that provide their food are highly sensitive to changes in water conditions. Sewage and fertilizers from human settlements flow down rivers into coastal waters, causing bacteria to multiply and remove oxygen from the water. Deforestation and farming can discharge huge amounts of silt into rivers that carry it out to sea, smothering the coral.

Scientists have discovered that global warming is adding to the stresses on coral reefs. A rise of 2–4°C (4–7°F) kills the algae that live within the coral polyps, causing "coral bleaching" – where the reef turns pale and slowly dies. Other damage to coral reefs is caused by oceans becoming more acidic as they absorb more carbon dioxide from the atmosphere.

Marine reserves

In 1960, the coral reefs of Florida Keys became the United States' first marine reserve, the John Pennekamp State Park. In 1998, the then US president, Bill Clinton, commissioned an environmental taskforce to examine threats to America's reefs and strengthen levels of protection. The taskforce defined two main areas of action:

1. to increase understanding of coral reefs by mapping their geography and conducting a comprehensive examination of reef species, and
2. to immediately reduce the impact of human activities on reef ecosystems, by extending protected areas and reducing the impact of pollution, mining, and trade in reef species.

The Great Barrier Reef off Australia's north-east coast is the world's largest coral reef, stretching for 2,000 kilometres (1,240 miles). The Barrier Reef Marine Park was set up in 1975 to preserve this rich marine ecosystem. Expanded in 2004, it now covers 345,000 square kilometres (133,200 square miles) – one of the world's largest marine reserves.

Coral reef conservation

Around 450,000 square kilometres (174,000 square miles) of coral reefs are protected worldwide. Commercial fishing, boat traffic, and pollution are regulated or outlawed on marine reserves. International treaties also guard against pollution. However, no conservation measures can protect reefs from the effects of global warming, and coral bleaching remains a major threat to reefs worldwide.

WHY CONSERVE WILDLIFE?

In addition to habitat loss and climate change, hunting, disease, and the introduction of non-**native** species are all serious threats to wildlife. Ecologists and environmental organizations are working to assess the risks and conserve rare species.

Hunting

Over-extraction, or hunting, presents a serious risk to many kinds of wildlife. Since prehistoric times, animals have been hunted for food, fur, feathers, shells, tusks, and other body parts. When there were few people and weapons were spears and arrows, hunting had little effect on animal populations, but the invention of the rifle stacked the odds in favour of hunters.

Nowadays, farming, rather than hunting, provides our food in the developed world. However, animals are still being hunted for meat in places such as Africa. In addition, big cats, elephants, and rhinos are killed for their fur or tusks, often illegally. Animals are also killed for sport. By the 20th century, sport hunting caused the extinction of a South African antelope called the bluebuck and the American passenger pigeon. Many migratory birds are still killed every year by sport hunters as they cross the Mediterranean. In addition, some dangerous or poisonous animals are killed out of fear, or hunted down as pests.

Protection against hunting

By the late 19th century, environmentalists realized that hunting was driving species such as the bison to extinction. They advised governments to take action, and by the 1960s and 70s, many countries had passed laws to protect rare species. In the United States, the Endangered Species Preservation Act was passed in 1966 to protect 78 species; now, as the Endangered Species Act, it covers over 1,300 species. In the 1970s and 1980s, environmental groups campaigned to publicize the plight of endangered species, such as whales. Sport hunting still goes on for species that are not endangered: the killing of animals such as moose, deer, ducks, and pheasants is permitted in certain seasons to licensed hunters.

Wildlife trade

Many types of animals and plants are worth far more alive than dead. Parrots and songbirds, stick insects, reptiles, and even baby apes are captured from the wild and sold as pets.

Plant species such as cactuses and orchids are threatened by collectors. In the 1990s, the trade in live animals and wildlife products was boosted by the invention of the internet. National laws and international agreements outlaw the trade in endangered species, but many species are still at risk from poachers.

Canadian hunters drag a dead harp seal to their boat. Many environmentalists protested when the Canadian government licensed fur hunters to kill 270,000 harp seals in 2008.

Fighting the fur trade

In the 1970s and 80s, environmental and animal rights groups launched campaigns against the fur trade. At the time, garments made from the fur of seals, foxes, mink, and otters were fashionable, posing a risk to some species. Greenpeace released images of baby seals being clubbed to death. These shocked audiences worldwide. An animal rights group called Lynx ran an advertising campaign to expose the reality behind the fur trade's glamorous image. These campaigns succeeded in convincing many people it was wrong to kill animals for their fur, and fur sales plummeted. In 1983, the European Union banned the import of fur from baby seals.

ENVIRONMENTALISM IN ACTION

Save the whale

Whales were once abundant throughout the world's oceans. For centuries, whalers in small boats, using hand-held harpoons, had hunted whales offshore. In the 17th century, whaling began to grow into a major industry. Whales were targeted for their meat and blubber, which was used to fuel oil lamps.

In the 19th century, the invention of steam engines and explosive harpoon guns made whaling more efficient, and whalers now pursued their quarry through the high seas. Whale oil was used to lubricate engines; ambergris from whale stomachs was used to make perfume; and bony **baleen** was used in corsets, umbrellas, and brushes.

When great whales such as blue, grey, and fin whales became scarce in the northern oceans, the whaling operations moved south. By the 1960s, a total of 60,000 whales were being killed annually. By this stage, many of the great whales were on the brink of extinction, and commercial whaling was no longer viable in many waters.

Campaign against whaling

In the mid-1970s, the newly formed environmental group Greenpeace launched a campaign against whaling. Greenpeace decided that the best way to bring attention to the plight of whales was through direct, non-violent action.

Greenpeace activists in flimsy rubber boats confronted the whaling ships. They were often hosed with high-power water jets for their pains. Film and photos of these stand-offs made headline news worldwide and convinced large numbers of people that whaling was wrong. They joined environmental groups, took part in demonstrations, and lobbied governments to ban whaling.

Ban on whaling

Following further lobbying by environmentalists, the Indian Ocean was declared a sanctuary for whales in 1979. In 1982, the International Whaling Commission voted to ban whaling. The ban came into effect in 1986. Antarctic waters became a whale sanctuary in 1994.

In 2001, Japanese whalers hosed Greenpeace activists as they monitored the slaughter of a minke whale off the coast of Antarctica.

Not all nations supported the ban on whaling. In the 1990s and 2000s, Japan and Iceland continued to hunt whales. Japan has killed 24,000 whales since the ban in 1986, with whale meat sold commercially in Japanese markets. Norway also continues to hunt whales, as it says it has done so for thousands of years. In addition, **indigenous** peoples worldwide, from the Inuit of the Arctic to the Maori of New Zealand, assert their right to hunt whales as part of their traditional culture.

Environmentalism has had a huge impact on the whaling industry, but 25 years after the ban came into effect, many of the great whales are still endangered. Sperm and bottlenose whales are now reasonably plentiful, and grey whales are slowly increasing, but blue, humpback, and fin whales have hardly increased in decades. Scientists fear that these whales are now too scarce for them to breed successfully. Meanwhile, Japan and Norway are pressing for the whaling ban to be lifted. In 2006, commercial whaling was started again, on a limited scale, by Iceland. Threatened by global warming, pollution, and overfishing, which **depletes** their food stocks, these ocean giants are still far from safe.

ENVIRONMENTALISM IN ACTION

The work of the IUCN

Set up in 1948, the International Union for Conservation of Nature (IUCN) is an international federation of conservation organizations, including government agencies and wildlife charities. It gathers data on rare species, works with countries worldwide to preserve wildlife, and promotes sustainable use of natural resources.

Since 1994, the IUCN has published its Red List of Threatened Species. This is a comprehensive list of species at risk worldwide. The List aims to raise awareness of conservation issues and guide conservation efforts around the world.

What is the Red List?

The Red List classifies animals and plants in seven categories according to their risk of extinction (see diagram). In 2011, the IUCN listed over 19,000 species of animals and plants as officially threatened with extinction, including polar bears, hippos, mountain gorillas, and tigers. However, only a tiny fraction – just 3 per cent – of all species have been assessed, so the true total is very much higher. According to the IUCN, the greatest concentration of threatened species occurs in densely populated areas in the tropics, including in forests, and on islands and mountains.

This diagram shows the Red List classification of species according to level of risk.

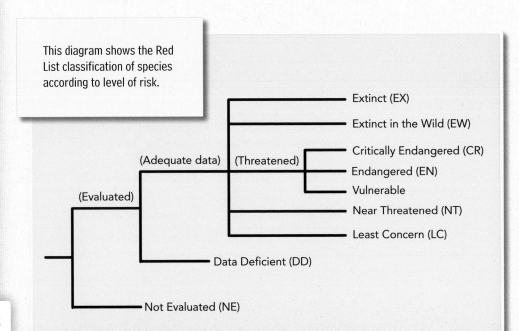

In 1973, the IUCN drafted the Convention on International Trade in Endangered Species (CITES). By 2011, 175 countries had signed the treaty. The aim is to promote international cooperation in regulating the trade in living plants and animals, and in wildlife products such as leather goods, furs, turtle shells, and medicines. This is done by issuing licences only to authorized traders. Trade in threatened plants and animals is tightly controlled, while trade in endangered species is banned.

Unfortunately, the rarer the species, the higher the price it commands on the illegal market. Despite CITES and national laws, rare plants and animals are still traded illegally, and endangered species such as rhinos and big cats are still killed for their horns or fur. In countries where poverty and hunger are widespread, people are prepared to risk fines, imprisonment, injury, or even death for the chance to earn big money from the sale of a leopard skin or rhino horn.

The Red List and river dolphins

The family Platanistidae (or river dolphin) contains just four living species that inhabit rivers and estuaries. These intelligent mammals are threatened by habitat loss, pollution, and hunting – with some species being killed simply to provide fish bait. The Red List classifies the Ganges and Indus river dolphins as endangered, and the La Plata dolphin as vulnerable.

Not enough data is available to classify the Amazon river dolphin (shown here). A fifth species, the Chinese river dolphin, is listed as critically endangered. All species are legally protected, but this is difficult to enforce in remote areas such as the Amazon, where people may not even be aware of the law.

Introduced species

Introduced species are non-native plants and animals that have been brought to new habitats by humans. For centuries, people have introduced alien species as we have colonized new areas.

Helpful and harmful impacts

A great many introductions have been beneficial – at least to humans. For example, in the 16th century, European settlers introduced crops such as wheat, rice, potatoes, and sugar cane to new areas worldwide. These crops now provide much of the world's food. Livestock such as cattle, sheep, pigs, and chickens were widely introduced for food. Honey bees, originally from Asia, now provide honey and pollinate plants throughout the settled world.

However, some introductions that were not well planned have proved disastrous for people, native wildlife, and even whole ecosystems. Introduced plant-eaters such as cattle and sheep destroy vegetation, while non-native predators such as rats, cats, and dogs prey on native species.

Not all introductions are deliberate. Rats, snakes, and other species have arrived as accidental stowaways on planes, ships, and trucks – and have sometimes wreaked havoc in their new homes. A type of shellfish called the zebra mussel, originally from south-west Europe, reached new regions in ships' **ballast**. In waterways such as North America's Great Lakes, it now dominates lakebed ecosystems, out-competing native shellfish.

Introduced animals often have a particularly harmful impact on island ecosystems. In the 17th and 18th centuries, European sailors routinely left livestock such as goats and pigs on remote islands to provide food for when they returned. Food and space on islands are limited, and the introduced livestock often overgrazed whole islands. New predators such as rats and cats hunted native island wildlife to extinction.

Control of invasive species

Introduced species are generally hardy survivors that breed quickly. By the time people realize they are pests, they are well established. They are then very difficult – and expensive – to remove. Methods used to control invasive animals include trapping, baiting, and **culling** by rifle. Native species threatened by new predators may have to be taken to reserves that can be fenced to keep out intruders. Many countries now have strict **biosecurity** measures to prevent further introductions. People and cargo arriving by air, sea, rail, or road are scanned electronically or inspected by sniffer dogs, and non-native species are removed.

A national biosecurity authority was founded in Australia in 2008. This sniffer dog is carrying out a quarantine inspection for fruit and other forbidden items in bags at Sydney airport.

Then and Now
Introduced species in New Zealand

The islands of New Zealand were isolated for millions of years. This allowed many unique species to evolve there, including flightless birds such as kiwis. There were very few native predators. In the 19th century, Europeans introduced hundreds of alien plants, and mammals such as cats, rats, and weasels. These preyed on flightless birds and their eggs. Introduced livestock such as deer, sheep, and pigs caused widespread soil erosion. New Zealand now spends large sums of money **eradicating** non-native predators and conserving native wildlife.

ENVIRONMENTALISM IN ACTION

Controlling invasive species in Australia

The continent of Australia has been separate from other landmasses for 200 million years. Many unique animals evolved there, including marsupials such as kangaroos and possums, and egg-laying platypuses. **Endemic** (unique) species include amphibians, reptiles, birds, and thousands of plants.

Some 50,000 years ago, the Aboriginal people reached the continent, bringing with them a type of wild dog called the dingo, which became the top predator. In the 19th century, European colonists introduced hundreds of new plants. Domestic stock such as sheep, cattle, goats, and pigs were imported and bred for food. Camels, horses, and buffalo were also introduced. Non-native predators such as dogs, cats, and rats were soon preying on native wildlife.

Problem pests

Rabbits were introduced from Europe in the 1850s to provide food and sport hunting. They multiplied rapidly and, within 30 years, had reached plague proportions in many areas. Colonists tried to control rabbits by releasing European red foxes, but the foxes did more harm to native species than to rabbits. In 1950 the Australian government tried to eradicate rabbits by introducing the disease myxomatosis, but rabbit populations soon recovered. There are currently more than 200 million rabbits in Australia. Control measures include installing and maintaining thousands of kilometres of rabbit-proof fences to preserve grazing land, at great expense.

Cane toads

In 1935, another planned introduction proved disastrous. Cane toads were brought from South America to control beetles that were destroying sugar cane crops in Queensland. These large, poisonous amphibians bred quickly and spread beyond the cane fields, preying on native reptiles, frogs, and small mammals. There are now 200 million of these large toads, and measures such as culling and trapping have met with limited success.

Impact on wildlife

Alien species threaten the survival of Australian wildlife such as numbats and bandicoots, two groups of smallish, once-widespread marsupials. The bilby, or rabbit-eared bandicoot, feeds on seeds and roots – but rabbits are now monopolizing its food sources, and it is killed by predators. The lesser bilby is extinct and the greater bilby is vulnerable.

Bilbies are small, nocturnal marsupials of the Australian Outback. This rare species is now protected by fenced enclosures in special wildlife reserves.

Control measures

Management and control of invasive species are a key part of environmental policy in Australia. The government says: "It would be desirable to rid Australia of its worst invasive species, but this is not achievable in most cases". Vast sums are spent reducing numbers of pests, and eradicating them entirely from offshore island reserves. From time to time, bounties (rewards) are offered for killing dingoes, dogs, cats, and foxes, which helps to reduce their numbers. This practice is opposed by some animal-rights groups.

Control of non-native weeds costs A$3.5 billion a year, and new diseases and fungi that harm crops are also major problems. Of course, not all non-native species are regarded as pests. Introduced crops and livestock such as sheep and cattle provide Australia with much of its food and income from exports.

NATURE CONSERVATION

National parks and nature reserves are areas set aside for the conservation of habitats and wildlife. But they are also established for public recreation, with most parks encouraging visitors. Some protected areas are home to many thousands of people. Park authorities have to balance the needs of wildlife, visitors, and local people.

National parks and reserves

National parks and reserves are usually set up to protect areas of outstanding beauty or biodiversity. Many have spectacular natural features or unusual geology, such as hot springs or volcanoes. In the United States and most other countries, the land is owned by the nation. US parks are run by the National Park Service, set up in 1916. In the United Kingdom, most parkland is privately owned, although public bodies such as the National Trust may own some land. Each UK park is run by a National Parks Authority (NPA), headed by a committee made up of local people and government officers.

The aims of national parks and reserves

The main objectives of national parks and reserves are to conserve nature, but also to allow public access and recreation – for people to enjoy nature and get to know it better. These two main aims sometimes conflict with one another. Parks designated as wilderness areas may have a policy of restricting visitor numbers – for example, by charging high entry fees and issuing limited numbers of permits. This is sometimes called "fortress conservation". Elsewhere, visitors are encouraged, not least because the money they bring in is used to fund conservation.

Park authorities must also manage natural resources, such as timber and minerals. Mining is usually forbidden and development kept to a minimum. Rangers are employed to run the park, provide information, and look after wildlife and people. Scientists such as ecologists and biologists are employed to preserve biodiversity and advise on conservation. Forests are generally managed sustainably, with replanting to restore areas where timber is harvested. However, in countries such as Brazil and Indonesia, illegal logging in parks is a problem.

Then and Now
The Kinder Trespass

Britain had no national parks before the 1950s. Up until this time, the countryside was mainly owned by private landowners who would **evict** walkers who entered to enjoy the scenery. Surrounded by cities, the Peak District in Derbyshire became the focus of a campaign for people's right to enjoy the countryside. In 1932, 500 walkers trespassed onto the moor and held a protest on a hill called Kinder Scout. Five walkers were arrested and sent to prison. But the Kinder Scout Trespass became a milestone in the fight to gain access to the countryside. In 1951, the Peak District became Britain's first national park. It now receives 22 million visitors a year. Sadly, Kinder Scout now suffers from erosion caused by the feet of so many walkers on the main paths that lead through the park. The public are asked to stick to the trails to reduce erosion.

The Peak District National Park protects 1,437 square kilometres (555 square miles) of moorland, farmland, villages, and towns.

Providing for visitors

Parks cater for tourists by providing facilities such as information centres, toilets, shops, and restaurants. Most parks provide some form of accommodation, whether in hotels, hostels, refuges, or campsites. Since most people arrive by car, there must be car parks. However, most authorities discourage the use of cars within the park because it causes pollution. People are encouraged to leave their cars and explore on foot, horseback, or by bike. Many parks provide for a wide range of recreational activities, such as hang-gliding, white-water rafting, caving, fishing, canoeing, and diving. However, the authorities must make sure that these activities do not detract from other people's quiet enjoyment of the place.

Tourist management in the Lake District

The English Lake District in Cumbria protects a highly scenic area of lakes, hills, and mountains west of the M6 motorway. Covering nearly 2,300 square kilometres (900 square miles), the park receives over 15 million visitors a year. The authorities manage these large numbers by distinguishing between areas developed for tourism and quieter areas. Two main access routes from the M6 link to the park's main towns, Keswick, Ambleside, and Windermere. These towns and the surrounding area have been developed for tourism, with shops, restaurants, car parks, hotels, and caravan sites. Roads have been upgraded to avoid congestion. Three regions on the edges of the park are managed as quiet areas, with far fewer facilities. Many roads here have been preserved as country lanes. These areas receive fewer visitors so nature is left mainly undisturbed.

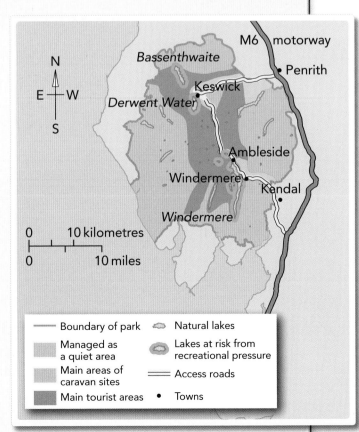

Managing tourists

The most popular national parks receive millions of visitors a year. The authorities have to manage visitors carefully, so that large numbers of tourists do not spoil the very peace and beauty people come to enjoy. The most scenic areas may suffer from overcrowding. Paths and wild areas may be eroded by walkers, cyclists, and horses, so in some parks, visitors are confined to specially prepared walkways. Litter is a major problem in some parks, including in remote places such as Mount Everest. In many parks, gangs of volunteers are organized regularly to clean up litter.

Populations in parks

In some parts of the world, national parks and reserves are mainly wilderness areas with very few people. For example, Grand Canyon National Park in Arizona, USA, covers 4,930 square kilometres (1,900 square miles) but only has about 1,000 inhabitants. By contrast, UK parks have been established in settled areas with many towns and villages. For example, the Peak District National Park has 38,000 inhabitants and includes several sizeable towns. The main activity in UK parks is farming, but there is also some manufacturing, mining, and quarrying. Energy must be generated and domestic waste disposed of. In UK parks, the authorities have extra duties: to preserve the local economy and provide jobs and housing. Sustainable development is now seen as the key to preserving prosperity and jobs while safeguarding nature. The NPA says: "Our parks are not museums to nature and contain many real working communities".

Some resorts in European parks, such as Wengen in the Swiss Alps, are car-free.

ENVIRONMENTALISM IN ACTION

Visitor management in Yosemite National Park

Yosemite National Park in California, USA, covers 3,100 square kilometres (1,200 square miles) of mountain scenery sculpted by glaciers, including sheer cliffs, waterfalls, and lakes. The naturalist John Muir visited the area in the 1860s and campaigned for its protection. Thanks to Muir's enthusiasm, Yosemite was given to the state of California in 1864 for "public use, resort, and recreation", becoming America's first protected area. It became a national park in 1890.

By the 1950s, Yosemite had become a popular tourist destination. Tourism was concentrated in an area of scenic beauty, the Yosemite Valley. Here visitors could enjoy the spectacular scenery, and also activities such as horseriding, fishing, climbing, cycling, rafting, golf, tennis, and swimming. During the 1980s, 80 per cent of park visitors stayed overnight, mostly in rooms, cabins, and campsites at Curry Village in the valley.

Impact of tourism

Yosemite Valley constitutes just 1 per cent of the park's total area, leaving most of the rest undeveloped, and conforming to the concept of wilderness as defined by the US government: "an area where the earth and its community of life are untrammelled by man, where man himself is a visitor who does not remain". However, within the valley tourism was causing considerable harm to the environment.

Infrastructure such as restaurants, accommodation, roads, and car parks had caused habitat loss. Visitors were eroding beauty spots and creating noise that disturbed wildlife. Despite a free bus service linking the main sights, many people were still using cars, causing congestion and pollution. Smoke and fumes from campfires and car exhausts sometimes resulted in smog, which damaged plants. In the 1990s, overnight accommodation was reduced to minimize disturbance to nature. By 2000, only 20 per cent of visitors were staying overnight. However, this only increased the number of daily car journeys and the resulting pollution.

A new plan

By 2000, Yosemite was receiving 4 million visitors a year. New resorts and businesses just outside the park boundaries were eating into wild habitats. The Sierra Club announced: "In the last 15 years, Americans have nearly loved Yosemite to death, their swelling numbers causing gridlock and smog". Environmentalists put forward a plan to restore some of the valley's wildness. The plan calls for overnight accommodation in the park to be reduced still further. It aims to tackle pollution and congestion by relocating car parks to a central area or outside the park, and requiring visitors to use buses. The aim is to reduce commercialization within the valley. However, development is likely to increase just outside the park, endangering surrounding habitats and their wildlife.

Then and Now
The Yosemite Firefall

The Yosemite Firefall was a nightly summer ritual dating back to 1872. Burning embers were dropped over a high cliff called Glacier Point overlooking the Valley, to create a "waterfall" of fire. The National Park Service banned the Firefall in 1968 because it attracted huge numbers of visitors and was not a natural event.

Hikers enjoy Yosemite's towering redwood trees and the 739-metre (2,425-foot) Yosemite Falls.

Tourism and conservation

The tourist industry dates back to the 19th century. In the 20th century, it grew faster than any other industry, with the development of mass tourism, including package tours, cruises, ski holidays, and safaris. Package holidays became increasingly popular from the 1950s, following the arrival of cheap air travel, and holiday resorts sprang up on coasts worldwide. Tourism is now one of the world's most important industries, generating huge amounts of income and also employment. For many countries, it is the main earner. It has often provided the key to development in remote places. However, resorts in remote destinations are quite often owned by foreign businesses, so much of the profit goes abroad.

Impact on the natural world

Tourism has had a harmful impact on many ecosystems worldwide. Air travel is a major source of the **greenhouse gases** that are triggering climate change. The construction of resorts and infrastructure, such as roads, car parks, airports, railways, cable cars, ski-lifts, and boat marinas, causes damage to wild areas. Large numbers of tourists bring pollution, such as litter and sewage, while visitors' cars cause air pollution. In wild areas, tourists can disturb animals, while in many resorts tourism is overstretching natural resources, such as water.

Ecotourism

Ecotourism developed as an alternative to mass tourism in the 1980s, in the light of green thinking. Also known as responsible or sustainable tourism, it aims to minimize harm to nature while providing income for local people. It also aims to increase environmental awareness and provide funds for conservation. Ecotourism generally involves small groups visiting remote places. Eco-resorts minimize environmental harm by using **renewable** energy and recycling waste and water. Since 2000, ecotourism has expanded faster than any other form of tourism.

Most eco-tourist schemes have remained true to the twin aims of being environmentally friendly and helping local communities. However, a few companies have been accused of "**greenwashing**" – using the language of environmentalism to drum up custom while harming nature. Ecotourism still often involves air travel, which increases numbers of visitors to remote destinations and so damages the environment. Critics point out that much of the money from ecotourism still goes to foreign investors, with local people mainly employed in low-paid jobs.

Ecotourism in Uganda

Bwindi Impenetrable National Park in Uganda is home to nearly half of the world's mountain gorillas. In the 20th century, the numbers of these great apes dropped steeply due to deforestation and hunting for meat and trophies. Baby apes were captured for sale as pets. The region was also disrupted by war, and the gorillas became critically endangered. Ecotourism in Bwindi is now helping to conserve these rare animals. Limited numbers of visitors are taken on guided tours to view gorillas from a safe distance. However, even limited contact with humans may stress the animals, so ecotourism is not a perfect solution. Some conservationists fear that the gorillas are losing their natural fear of humans, which makes them more vulnerable to poachers.

A young gorilla with an adult male in Bwindi National Park. Visitors' fees are used to fund conservation and guard against poachers.

ENVIRONMENTALISM IN ACTION

Conservation and the Maasai

The Great Rift Valley in East Africa is famous for its wildlife. Tourists flock to national parks and reserves here to spot Africa's "big five" most popular animals — lion, leopard, elephant, buffalo, and rhino – and also zebra, giraffe, and antelope. However, these savannah grasslands in southern Kenya and northern Tanzania are also the traditional lands of the Maasai. For centuries, this semi-nomadic people have grazed their herds of cattle, goats, and sheep here. Livestock are their main source of status and income.

The idea of land ownership is alien to Maasai culture. Since the middle of the 20th century, land ownership deals have deprived the Maasai of traditional grazing lands. Surprisingly, the biggest losses have been caused by conservation. Seventy per cent of parks and reserves in the region have been set up on Maasai lands. Tourism and conservation are the only activities allowed in national parks. The Maasai are forbidden to graze their livestock. This deprives them of their livelihood as well as their land.

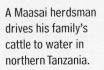

A Maasai herdsman drives his family's cattle to water in northern Tanzania.

Amboseli National Park

Amboseli (meaning "place of water") in southern Kenya is an area with freshwater springs and swamps where the Maasai traditionally watered their livestock. The region's biodiversity was recognized in 1948 when it became a reserve. In 1974, the Kenyan government decided to increase the protection level by declaring it a national park. This decision was taken after discussion with local politicians and the Maasai. New national parks in developing countries are established with the help of funds from international conservation organizations. The funds are partly used to develop infrastructure needed for tourism, which will be an important new source of foreign cash. However, local people who are forced off their land often receive little compensation.

The Maasai were promised compensation for loss of grazing land in Amboseli, to be paid annually, and a new pipeline so they could water their stock outside the park. However, the pipeline was inefficient and the payments stopped after three years. At an international conference in 2004, a Maasai spokesman declared that conservation had displaced 100,000 Maasai. Since traditional grazing practices maintained the region's biodiversity, his people were "the original conservationists. Now you have made us enemies of conservation".

Conservation organizations such as the IUCN declare their support and respect for local cultures, but this does not always result in practical support and compensation for loss of land and livelihood. Critics say that all too often, the initiative to set up protected areas comes from organizations in the developed world and politicians in distant cities, with little discussion with local people.

Environmental organizations, such as Friends of the Earth and WWF, stress that all new conservation initiatives should recognize local land rights and involve indigenous peoples. In 2005, the Kenyan government announced that Amboseli's national park status would be downgraded to that of a national reserve, which would be run by the county council and the Maasai. Reserves have more flexible rules about activities such as herding. Some conservation organizations were alarmed by this move, but others welcomed it as an important step in recognizing Maasai rights and involving them in conservation.

ENVIRONMENTALISM IN ACTION

Work of the WWF on Madagascar

Madagascar is the world's fourth-largest island. Situated off the east coast of Africa, it covers 587,042 square kilometres (226,658 square miles). It is an area incredibly rich in biodiversity, with many endemic plants and animals – species unknown elsewhere. For example, Madagascar has 10,000 plant species, of which 75 per cent are unique. Over 90 per cent of the island's reptiles are endemic, including 50 types of chameleons. Unique mammals include 100 species of primates called lemurs. However, a great many species are now threatened with extinction.

The northern giant mouse lemur was recognized as a species in 2005, following genetic research by German scientists. Not enough data is available to assess its conservation status.

Until a few centuries ago, this long, mountainous island was almost entirely wooded. However, around 2,000 years ago, the island was colonized by settlers from Indonesia. Indonesian farmers traditionally clear patches of forest for farming or fuel using a slash-and-burn technique that they call *tavy*. Trees are felled and burned, and the forest then grows back. However, Madagascar's unique forests grew back only very slowly, if at all.

European settlers in the 16th century began to cause further problems for wildlife by introducing new predators, and through mining operations. During the 20th century, the Madagascan population grew very rapidly. By 2010, the island had over 20 million inhabitants. Most people are poor and depend on *tavy* to grow crops and raise livestock.

Madagascar has lost 90 per cent of its forests since 1900, leaving only relatively small pockets of untouched land. Without tree roots to hold the soil in place, deforestation has caused widespread erosion. In the 1990s, satellite pictures showed streams of red soil leaking into the ocean from all sides of the island. This soil then damaged aquatic ecosystems. Experts estimate that many of Madagascar's unique species are endangered by deforestation, introductions of alien species, and hunting – both for meat and live trading. Endemic plants and animals are taken from the wild illegally and sold abroad.

Conservation on Madagascar

WWF has been working in Madagascar for 30 years to preserve remaining forests and their wildlife. The charity works through community-based projects run by and involving local people. Conservation work on the island recognizes the need and right of local people to earn a living from their land. This is accomplished by making local people partners in conservation, and providing training in sustainable use of natural resources.

In the 1980s, WWF experts surveyed Madagascar's habitats and assessed the threats to biodiversity. In the 1990s, the organization provided funding to protect biodiverse habitats. Over 200 sites were protected with the cooperation of local groups. In 1997, it helped to launch an ecology training programme (ECT) to train local scientists, ecologists, and conservation experts. ECT graduates have made important discoveries, including of many new species.

Since 2000, WWF has launched new initiatives to promote sustainable development. It has negotiated a ban on mining while new protected areas are developed. Ecotourism and sustainable projects such as forestry and butterfly farming are helping to halt deforestation. However, rare habitats are still under intense pressure from the rising human population.

WILDLIFE CONSERVATION

Species that are very rare are classed as "critically endangered". When just a few hundred individuals are left, the species will probably die out if nothing is done to help it. Measures such as protecting habitats, reducing pollution, providing legal protection, captive breeding, and removing predators are used to save threatened species. Conservation can only be effective if supported by local people – but sometimes human needs conflict with the needs of wildlife.

Assessing needs

The first step in trying to save an endangered species is to assess its numbers, and also its needs such as habitat, food, and breeding. Modern technology such as genetic monitoring may be used to assess numbers. Scientists collect samples like dung in the field, use them to identify the species that left them, and then use the information to estimate the local population. Genetic monitoring has even led to the discovery of new species, such as a previously unknown monitor lizard and several small lemurs.

Animals may be tagged, ringed, or fitted with radio transmitters to track their movements. Ecologists need to fully understand a species' role in its environment – its relationships to other living things that provide its food or prey upon it – before being able to make plans to meet its needs.

Captive breeding

Since the 1950s, captive breeding programmes have saved rare species such as the California condor from extinction. In the 1980s, only about 20 of these birds remained in the wild. In a controversial programme, scientists captured the remaining birds and bred them. About 180 have since been released into the wild.

Animals can only be released if a suitable habitat is found, which can be very difficult in the case of large creatures that need a lot of space, such as elephants. Scientists also fear that small populations have little genetic variation, which makes the species vulnerable to disease.

Captive breeding programmes are very expensive, with much of the money raised by donation to environmental groups. The condor programme has cost $35 million. Some environmentalists say that this money would be better spent trying to save whole ecosystems rather than a single species.

Large, spectacular, or appealing animals such as pandas, snow leopards, and orang-utans attract funds through sponsorship programmes whereby people are encouraged to "adopt" an animal. It is much harder to generate money to save small, less appealing creatures such as insects. However, some experts believe that conservation money should be concentrated on efforts to save ecologically important species, such as bees (many species of which are in decline), that play a key role in ecosystems by pollinating plants.

The giant panda is a symbol of conservation. These mammals are threatened by habitat loss and poaching. Since the 1950s, the Chinese government has spent huge sums on a captive breeding programme.

ENVIRONMENTALISM IN ACTION

Conserving the wildlife of Hawaii

The Hawaiian Islands are a remote chain in the centre of the Pacific, with eight large islands and 124 smaller ones. These steep-sided volcanic islands are covered with dense tropical forest, and are rich in biodiversity and unique species. For example, some 50 species of birds called honeycreepers have evolved from a single species that reached the islands. These birds evolved differently shaped beaks to suit different diets, such as nectar and insects.

An incredible variety of fungi, mosses, ferns, flowering plants, insects, snails, and birds evolved on Hawaii, but no land reptiles or amphibians reached the islands. The only large mammal to visit was the monk seal. Ninety-five per cent of all native plants and 99 per cent of insects and snails are endemic.

Human impact

About 1,600 years ago, Hawaii was colonized by Polynesians, who introduced sugar cane, bananas, breadfruit, and small pigs. In the 19th century, Europeans brought sheep, cattle, goats, and large pigs. Rats arrived as stowaways, dogs and cats as pets, and later mongooses were introduced to control rats. These alien predators wiped out flightless birds. Mosquitoes, accidentally introduced in the 1820s, brought avian 'flu, which has reduced honeycreeper numbers.

By the 20th century, many forests had been felled. Since then, many lowland and coastal habitats have been lost to farming and tourist resorts. Introduced plants have crowded out native plants, and wildlife habitats have been damaged by **feral** livestock – especially pigs. Since the first settlers arrived in Hawaii, thousands of unique species have died out, including many types of tree snail and 20 species of flightless bird.

Hawaii became a US state in 1959. It is often called the endangered species capital of the United States with a third of all the country's species listed as threatened.

Conservation

Since the 1950s, conservation has been a high priority on Hawaii. Initiatives include removing non-native species such as mongooses, cats, rats, and the predatory Jackson's chameleon, which escaped from captivity.

Endangered birds such as honeycreepers have been bred in captivity. Large sums have been spent trying to reduce the numbers of highly destructive pigs. However, culling pigs is unpopular with islanders who like to hunt them for meat and sport. The animal has an important role in Hawaiian culture.

Since it has proved impossible to eradicate pigs from the dense forests, reserves are often fenced to protect native plants. Some reserves are also off-limits for visitors. Non-native plants are destroyed and the land replanted with native vegetation. Strict biocontrol methods at ports and airports prevent the introduction of new alien species.

Then and Now
The nene

The Hawaiian goose, or nene (seen here), has been the subject of a successful breeding programme. Around 250,000 of these birds are believed to have existed in 1800, but their numbers were reduced by hunting and introduced predators. By 1951, just 30 geese remained. They were captured and bred on two reserves, in Hawaii and on the Slimbridge Reserve in the United Kingdom, under a programme directed by leading UK conservationist Sir Peter Scott. The nene bred well in captivity. About 1,500 have been released in Hawaii and the bird is off the immediate danger list.

Sport hunting and conservation

Many people think that humans should not hunt and kill animals for pleasure. Deep ecologists see hunting as a violation of animals' rights. Yet the first protected areas were game reserves.

In medieval times, European kings and Indian landowners set aside reserves to hunt deer, boar, or tigers. Ordinary people were not allowed to hunt there, only noblemen and their guests. These reserves were established out of love of hunting, not for conservation. Yet they had the effect of conserving whole ecosystems. They also provided employment for gamekeepers and stewards, who had to ensure that there was plenty of healthy game. The hunting was limited because of the relatively small numbers of hunters who were only permitted to hunt in certain seasons.

Many national parks and nature reserves started out as game reserves. For example, the New Forest in southern Britain was set up to hunt deer by William the Conquerer in 1079. Gran Paradiso in the European Alps was set aside for hunting in 1836. It became Europe's first national park in 1922. Many African parks originated as hunting grounds set up by white rulers in colonial times.

Modern trophy hunting

In the 19th and 20th centuries, hunting for food and sport increased in scale, causing the extinction of many species. The last African quagga, a species of zebra, was wiped out in the 1880s. The American passenger pigeon was wiped out in 1914. Elephants, black rhinos, and bison would probably have gone the same way, but for laws passed in the 20th century to protect endangered species.

Hunting is still strictly outlawed in most parks and reserves. However, in modern times, sport hunting has actually helped to preserve some species and their habitats. For example, a wildfowl-hunting group in North America called Ducks Unlimited has provided funds to restore wetland habitats. The aim is to increase stocks of ducks to provide better hunting, but habitat restoration helps to preserve all wetland species. During the hunting season, the Ducks Unlimited hunters are careful to limit the numbers of ducks that are shot, so that wildfowl do not decline.

Twenty-three countries in Africa now run game-hunting operations. The total area protected by these reserves actually exceeds the area protected by national parks. Trophy hunters from Europe, the United States, and Japan pay large sums of money to shoot lions, leopards, elephants, buffaloes, and rhinos in these reserves.

Local guides lead the hunters to their quarry and select particular animals – usually older males past their prime. In this way, hunting does not harm the breeding population. The legal African game industry is now worth £122 million a year.

Many environmentalists condemn the hunting of wild animals in confined spaces from which they cannot escape – a practice they call "canned hunting". They point out that many of the animals have been hand-reared, and so have no fear of humans and make very easy targets. However, a growing number of conservationists now believe that game hunting can play a part in protecting habitats and wildlife. They point out that the large sums generated by the industry encourage local people to conserve wildlife that might otherwise be vulnerable to poaching and illegal hunting. In Africa, sport hunting has helped to preserve threatened species such as the white rhino and black wildebeest.

An American teenager poses with an African eland she has killed. It is traditional for the hunter's face to be painted with the blood of the first animal he or she has killed.

ENVIRONMENTALISM IN ACTION

Can tigers be saved?

Tigers are top predators in dense tropical forests and wetlands. Once widespread throughout southern and south-east Asia, tigers are now endangered, mainly because of hunting and habitat loss. In places such as Indonesia and Malaysia, their forest habitats are being felled to make way for fields and plantations. The construction of roads, railways, towns, and mines is eating into forests and wetlands. Experts say that just 7 per cent of the tiger's historic habitat remains.

Tigers are hunted for their striped fur and for meat. Their bones and body parts are ground up and used in traditional Eastern medicine. In most areas, tigers are legally protected, but they are still killed by poachers. They are also hunted down when they enter settled lands to kill livestock, or even people. They are widely feared as man-eaters, and may kill about 60 people a year.

Experts estimate that there were 100,000 tigers in Asia in 1900. There are now just 3,200 – down by 97 per cent. Of nine subspecies alive in 1900, three are now extinct. The remaining six – Bengal, Indochinese, Malayan, Sumatran, Amur, and South China tigers – are all endangered or critically endangered.

Awe-inspiring Bengal tigers like this one have been symbols of conservation for decades.

Tiger conservation

In the 1970s, the WWF launched Project Tiger in India. It worked with the Indian government to set up reserves and ban tiger hunting. As a result, India's tiger population had doubled by 1990. However, despite conservation efforts, tiger numbers are still falling overall. In 2010, the year of the tiger in the Chinese calendar, WWF launched its Year of the Tiger campaign. The aim is to double existing tiger numbers by 2022, the next Chinese year of the tiger.

Thirteen countries where tigers live have pledged to work towards this goal, by establishing reserves and patrolling them against poachers. They will also support local tiger conservation efforts, and (with international cooperation) banning the illegal trade in tiger parts. However, growing human populations continue to invade tiger habitats. Each cat needs a large area in which to hunt, and as human populations expand rapidly in Asia, there is less and less space for tigers.

New tiger reserve

In 2004, with the aid of the Wildlife Conservation Society (WCS), the world's largest tiger reserve was established in the remote Hukawng Valley in northern Burma. It now covers around 22,000 square kilometres (8,450 square miles) and the WCS believes 50 tigers live in the valley. However, some environmentalists are concerned that the Burmese government is not fully committed to the project, since it has recently encouraged human settlement in the region. A decade ago, the opening of a highway brought a rush of gold seekers to this remote area. Gold mining causes pollution, and increased hunting for food has reduced stocks of boar and deer that provide food for tigers.

WCS has proposed that the most populated parts of the valley become "multi-use areas". Here fishing and **subsistence hunting** will be permitted. Livestock rearing will be encouraged, to reduce the need to hunt wild game. Sustainable crops such as bamboo and rattan will be harvested. Ecotourism will bring in foreign cash. However, Burma remains one of the world's poorest countries. One tiger skeleton is worth ten years' wages on the illegal market, so poaching will remain a threat in Hukawng.

Overfishing

Fish and shellfish have been a major source of food since prehistoric times. Early fishing boats kept to coastal waters, but since the 16th century, fishing fleets have also fished in open waters. In the 20th century new technology such as sonar and satellites helped fishermen to pinpoint shoals of fish. Modern "factory" trawlers are equipped with huge nets that can capture whole shoals at a time. The technique of flash freezing allows the trawlers to stay at sea for days and return with hundreds of tonnes of fish.

Today, 3.5 million fishing vessels ply the oceans. Around one per cent are industrial-scale trawlers which net 60 per cent of the world's catch. When so many fish are caught that not enough are left to breed, it is called overfishing. The late 20th century saw fish stocks plummet. Some fisheries collapsed entirely. In the 20th century the cod fishery off Newfoundland, Canada collapsed with the loss of 40,000 jobs.

The fishing industry also involves a lot of waste. About one-quarter of the world's total catch is **"by-catch"** – unwanted species such as dolphins, sharks, turtles, and seabirds that are thrown back dead or dying. Environmentalists and many other people feel this is a terrible waste of natural resources, while the killing of top predators such as dolphins and sharks can have far reaching effects on marine food chains.

Overfishing causes hardship for fishing communities. It also impacts on marine ecosystems, including on fish-eating predators such as seabirds and dolphins, which then have no food to rear their young. By the late 20th century marine biologists and environmentalists realized that modern levels of fishing were unsustainable. Action was urgently needed to preserve fish stocks.

The Marine Stewardship Council (MSC) assesses fishing methods and awards sustainable operations with the blue MSC label.

At the World Summit on Sustainable Development in 2002, many nations agreed to restrict fishing in their coastal waters, and also limit their fishermen's catch. Unsurprisingly these limits, called **quotas**, are unpopular with fishermen. Some fleets have now moved to the open ocean where there are no regulations, to target deep-sea species such as toothfish. However, deep-sea fish are slow breeders and several of these new species being caught by fishermen are now also endangered.

Then and Now
Sustainable fishing in Bridlington

Bridlington, on Britain's north-east coast, was once a base for North Sea cod fishing. However, North Sea cod stocks declined steeply in the late 20th century. In 2006, conservation groups advised a total ban on cod fishing to allow stocks to recover. The people of Bridlington suffered when cod declined, but the port is now home to a small-scale, sustainable lobster industry. Following a voluntary code, fishermen take only large, mature lobsters. Smaller specimens and pregnant females are thrown back alive. These methods seem to be maintaining lobster stocks – in fact, the shellfish seem to be increasing, partly because there are fewer cod to eat their eggs.

Environmental groups urge shoppers to buy fish and other seafood such as lobsters from sustainable stocks.

WHAT IS THE FUTURE OF CONSERVATION?

A worldwide study called the Millennium Ecosystem Assessment took place in 2000. Over 1,300 scientists in 95 countries participated in a stock-take of the natural world. They concluded that habitats worldwide had changed more in the last 50 years than at any previous time in history. Sadly, a great many ecosystems are now being damaged by human activities, which are endangering thousands of species. IUCN scientists note that the greatest numbers of extinctions are taking place in densely populated countries that are industrializing fast, such as China, Indonesia, India, and Brazil. Habitat protection is now more important than ever.

Expansion of protected areas

Habitat protection has come a long way since the first parks were set up in the 1870s. The movement started quite slowly, but accelerated in the late 20th century. Six hundred protected areas were set up between 1900 and 1950. By 1960, there were 1,000. In 1990, the IUCN called for 10 per cent of each country's territory to be protected. Since that time, the total protected area has doubled, exceeding the IUCN target. However, roughly half of all land protected in the 20th century was either occupied or regularly used by humans. In some places, indigenous people have been put in charge of protected areas, but hundreds of thousands of people, such as the Maasai, have already been forced off their lands, creating great hardship and poverty.

People versus parks

It has never been easy to balance the needs of nature against human needs. In future, as populations expand, it will become even more difficult to achieve this balance. Yet just such a balance is vital if we are to continue to preserve the world's wild places. In future, the number of protected areas is likely to increase.

Conservationists are calling for "**wildlife corridors**" to be set up to link existing reserves, so that animals can move between them. At the same time, some major reserves are under threat, as pressure grows to make use of natural resources. For example, many US politicians now support plans to open the Arctic National Wildlife Refuge in Alaska to large-scale oil and gas extraction. Environmentalists say this would spell disaster for wildlife.

The Arctic National Wildlife Refuge protects 78,000 square kilometres (31,000 square miles) of the north Alaskan coast – home to species such as polar bear and caribou.

Sustainable development

Many conservationists feel that sustainable development offers a way forward for both people and wildlife. The pioneering 1992 Earth Summit conference held in Rio de Janeiro, Brazil, defined sustainable development as: "development that meets the needs of the present without compromising the ability of future generations to meet their own needs". As the human population rises, environmentalists say it is vital we learn to use Earth's natural resources sustainably – without wrecking the planet in the process. At the Rio Summit, 150 nations agreed that preserving Earth's biodiversity was a key part of sustainable development. The summit also concluded: "Local communities play a key role [in conservation] because they are the true managers of the ecosystems in which they live".

Climate change predictions

Most environmentalists believe that global warming is the most serious threat of modern times. Scientists predict that climate patterns will become more extreme, with drier areas becoming drier, and wet areas getting wetter. Droughts and violent storms will probably become more common. Violent weather events in the late 20th century and in the early 2000s suggest that these changes may already be starting to be seen.

Amphibians in danger

Amphibians seem to be more at risk from climate change than any other animal group, with the extinction of 168 frog species since 1980 from a variety of causes. In the Americas, 65 species of harlequin frogs have died out, while Australia has lost one whole genus (a sub-subfamily including all its species) of frogs. Amphibians lay their eggs in water, so they are threatened by the drying out of wetlands. According to the IUCN, 29 per cent of all 5,960 species of amphibians are endangered by climate change and pollution, while another 17 per cent are at risk of disease, mostly linked to drought.

The loss of sea ice habitat is the biggest threat to the survival of polar bears. A shorter sea ice season in southern Arctic regions has reduced the amount of time bears can hunt for their prey.

Impact of climate change

Over the next century, ecosystems worldwide are likely to feel the effects of climate change. Rising temperatures in the polar regions are causing the icecaps to melt in summer. This is affecting animals such as polar bears that hunt seals on the ice. As we have seen, rising temperatures are also harming coral reefs. Scientists predict that climate change could also alter ocean currents, which would affect whole marine ecosystems. Melting ice and warming oceans are causing sea levels to rise. In the future, rising sea levels could threaten wildlife living on coasts and islands worldwide, as well as over a billion people who live in coastal regions.

Global warming on land could cause deserts to expand. Meanwhile wetlands could dry out, threatening aquatic wildlife. Parts of the world's farmlands could become infertile. If this happened, farmers would have to exploit land that was previously wilderness, causing more habitat loss.

Tackling climate change

The climate is already changing, and there is overwhelming evidence that these changes are caused mostly be human activity. However, environmentalists say that much can be done to reduce the impact and slow the process down. Since the 1990s, the world's nations have met to try to reduce emissions of greenhouse gases that are causing climate change. At the Kyoto conference in 1997, many nations agreed to cut emissions, but some key nations, such as the United States, did not agree. Other nations, such as Switzerland and Austria, have failed to meet the targets they agreed to. The Copenhagen conference in 2009 failed to agree further reductions, although some voluntary reduction targets have been proposed by various countries since then.

Environmentalists say a new binding agreement on greenhouse gases is urgently needed. Meanwhile, they are calling on governments to invest in clean, renewable technologies that do not produce greenhouse gases. Campaigns by groups such as Friends of the Earth have helped people understand that everyday use of energy in cars, homes, at work, and at school is contributing to climate change. Every one of us can help to reduce the effects of global warming by using energy more carefully and efficiently.

ENVIRONMENTALISM IN ACTION

The future of Antarctica

Antarctica, Earth's fifth-largest continent, is a vast wilderness covered by an ice cap up to 4.5 kilometres (nearly 3 miles) thick. The climate inland is too hostile for living things, but penguins, seals, and seabirds thrive on the coasts. The Southern Ocean surrounding the continent is rich in life.

Antarctica was only discovered in the 1820s – and by the 1950s, seven nations had laid claim to parts of this enormous landmass. Some of these claims overlapped, which led to threats of war. The Antarctic Treaty of 1959 resolved the issue, and the countries concerned agreed to set aside their territorial claims. The treaty specified that Antarctica should be used only for scientific research – no development is allowed.

A German scientist measures air turbulence out on the Antarctic sea ice in 2005. His base was a research ship which could force its way through ice-choked seas.

In 1991, Antarctica and its surrounding waters became a wildlife reserve. Geologists believe that the continent holds rich reserves of minerals such as gold, silver, coal, and oil. However, a ban on mining is in place until at least 2048. Today Antarctica still has no permanent settlements. There are, however, research stations located mainly on coasts, staffed by about 1,000 scientists in winter and 5,000 in summer. Some 9,000 tourists visit the continent every year, but only very limited numbers are allowed ashore at any time to prevent wildlife being disturbed.

Antarctic scientists such as ecologists, marine biologists, and climatologists have made many important discoveries. Traces of pollution have been found in the air, ice, and oceans of even this remote wilderness, which provides information about how pollution spreads. In the 1980s Antarctic scientists discovered that the ozone layer in Earth's atmosphere was getting thinner. The cause was traced to pollutants called CFCs, used in some industrial processes and in household refrigerators and car air conditioning. CFCs have now been banned.

Threats to the polar regions

Global warming has had more impact on polar regions than on any other part of Earth. There has been significant melting in the Arctic, including the Greenland ice-sheets. A 3,250-square-kilometre (1,250-square-mile) chunk of ice broke off the ice-shelves edging Antarctica in 2002. Widespread melting could threaten Antarctic ecosystems, not least because it would affect the breeding cycle of a type of shrimp called krill, which is a major food source for seals, fish, birds, and whales. Krill, and fish such as the Patagonian toothfish (also known as Chilean sea bass), are also threatened by overfishing.

Conservation

Environmental groups such as WWF are working to regulate fishing in the Southern Ocean to protect rare fish species. They are also working to set up a network of marine protection areas (MPAs) in the Southern Ocean. In 2000, South Africa designated a new marine park covering 180,000 square kilometres (70,000 square miles) on the remote Prince Edward Islands. Environmentalists hope that MPAs covering a total of 2 million square kilometres (775,000 square miles) could help to reduce the effects of melting ice.

However, major action is required to significantly slow down global warming. That will need worldwide action at the local or regional level as well as international agreement, with millions of individual people taking practical steps to lessen their impact on the environment.

WHAT HAVE WE LEARNED?

Environmentalism is now over 150 years old. In the last century, the conservation movement has achieved an enormous amount. Thanks to conservationists, ecosystems rich in biodiversity such as coral reefs and rainforests have been preserved. National parks and reserves now protect many of the Earth's most beautiful landscapes. Without environmentalism, many plants and animals that have taken millions of years to evolve would have disappeared forever. There would probably be no great whales, pandas, elephants, or mountain gorillas. Lions, tigers, rhinos, and orang-utans would all have died out, and the world's oceans would have been much more severely overfished.

In the 20th century, environmental campaigners showed how pollution could damage ecosystems and harm wildlife. Thanks to pressure from green organizations, many countries passed laws to clean up habitats on land and water. In the late 20th century, environmentalists worked to convince people that global warming was a real and present threat. Governments, scientists, and millions of ordinary people around the world are now taking action to reduce the effects of climate change.

In the late 1990s, conservation groups such as the IUCN warned that the world was on the brink of a **mass extinction** caused by human activities, with species already disappearing at many times the natural rate. Environmentalists catalogued the main threats to wildlife: habitat loss, climate change, pollution, disease, hunting, and the introduction of new species. Environmental campaigners have raised billions of pounds to take action on these issues.

Humanity's duty of care

Environmentalism is about more than protecting habitats, saving wildlife, and reducing pollution. The movement has also shown that human beings are not separate from nature, but part of it. What is more, we cannot survive without it. The Convention on Biological Diversity, published in 1992, noted: "Biodiversity is in our self-interest. Biological resources are the pillars upon which we build civilizations ... The loss of biodiversity threatens our food supplies".

In the last 200 years or so, humans have spread to almost every part of the planet in ever-increasing numbers. Science and technology have allowed us to master the natural world. But environmentalists believe that with that mastery comes a duty to look after nature.

As the human population continues to increase – perhaps to 9 billion people within the next 30 years – environmentalists believe that sustainability provides the key to meeting human needs while preserving the planet. They also believe that it is vital to reduce poverty and hunger.

Future environmentalists will continue to work to convince people of the importance of conservation – not just for the sake of plants and animals, but also for our own survival. The Convention on Biological Diversity concludes: "Can we save the world's ecosystems, and with them the species we value? ... The answer will lie in our ability to bring our demands into line with nature's ability to produce what we need, and safely absorb what we throw away".

National parks such as Glen Canyon, USA were set up to protect spectacular scenery from development. However, parks will come under increasing pressure as the population expands.

TIMELINE

1079 William the Conquerer establishes the New Forest in southern Britain as a game reserve.

c.1700 The dodo is hunted to extinction on the island of Mauritius.

1836 Gran Paradiso in the Italian Alps is set aside for hunting.

1864 Yosemite in California becomes the United States' first protected area, being given to the state for "public use, resort, and recreation".

c.1870 Sport hunting causes the extinction of a type of zebra called the quagga.

1872 Yellowstone in the Rocky Mountains, USA becomes the world's first national park.

1890 Yosemite becomes a national park.

1892 US environmentalist John Muir founds the Sierra Club, a conservation organization.

1903 The first US National Bird Preserve is set up on Pelican Island, Florida – the start of the US Wildlife Refuge system.
Argentina's first reserve is established; it becomes a national park in 1934.

1905 The Audubon Society, a bird conservation society, is founded in the United States.

1914 Hunting causes the extinction of the passenger pigeon in the United States.

1916 The US National Park Service is set up.

1922 Gran Paradiso becomes Europe's first national park.

1932 500 British walkers campaign for people's right to enjoy the countryside by trespassing on Kinder Scout in the Peak District.

1948 The International Union for Conservation of Nature and Natural Resources (IUCN) is founded.

1951 The Nature Conservancy, an environmental organization, is founded in the United States.
The last 30 nene, or Hawaiian geese, are captured and bred on two reserves, in Hawaii and the United Kingdom.
The Peak District becomes the United Kingdom's first national park.

1959 The Antarctic Treaty suspends land claims to the continent and establishes that Antarctica is to be used only for peaceful scientific research.

1960 Part of Florida Keys becomes the first marine reserve in the United States.

1961 World Wildlife Fund (WWF) is founded.

1963 The Vanoise region in the Alps becomes the first French national park.

1969 Friends of the Earth is founded.

1970 Norwegian activist Arne Naess leads a protest against damming of the Mardalsfossen waterfall, later publishing his deep ecology philosophy.

1972 The Conference on the Human Environment, held in Sweden, is the first of a series of world environmental conferences.

1973 The International Union for Conservation of Nature drafts the Convention on International Trade in Endangered Species of Wild Fauna and Flora (CITES).
WWF launches Project Tiger in India.
Endangered Species Act is passed in the United States.

1974 Amboseli in southern Kenya becomes a national park.

1975 Greenpeace activists confront whaling ships to protest against whaling.
The Great Barrier Reef Marine Park is set up in Australia.

1979 The Indian Ocean becomes a sanctuary for whales.
Earth First!, an environmental group, is founded.

1982 The International Whaling Commission votes to ban whaling.

1983 The European Union bans the import of fur from baby seals.

1985 Rainforest Action Network is founded.
Greenpeace ship *Rainbow Warrior* is sunk in New Zealand by French agents, to prevent a Greenpeace anti-nuclear protest.

1987 A pioneering report on sustainable development, *Our Common Future*, is published by the Brundtland Commission.
The last Californian condors are captured and bred in captivity.

1991 Antarctica and the surrounding waters become a wildlife reserve.

1992 UN Earth Summit in Rio de Janeiro, Brazil, produces the Convention on Biological Diversity.
The cod fishery off Newfoundland collapses, with the loss of 40,000 jobs.

1994 Antarctic waters become a whale sanctuary.

1997 Kyoto climate conference; many nations agree to cut greenhouse gas emissions.

2000 Millennium Ecosystem Assessment takes place to assess the condition of Earth's ecosystems.

2005 Amboseli National Park in Kenya is downgraded to a reserve.

2008 A new 4,000-square-kilometre (1,100-square-mile) park is established in Guyana to protect a large area of untouched rainforest.

2010 The EU bans the import of illegally logged timber.

GLOSSARY

baleen bony material found in whales' mouths, used to filter food

ballast heavy material carried by a ship to provide stability

biodiversity variety of life in a particular habitat

biome habitat covering a large area, such as a desert

biosecurity safety measures that relate to living things

by-catch unwanted animals that are caught in fishermen's nets

conservation does not use up too many natural resources or pollute the environment

cull select and kill animals from a group

deep ecology radical form of environmentalism, which maintains the value of all living species for their own sake

deforestation when forest land is cleared of trees

degraded when a habitat or resource is damaged

deplete use up or exhaust a resource

ecologist scientist working in the field of ecology, which studies the interactions between living things and their environment

ecosystem web of life made up of all the living things in a habitat together with the soil, air, and conditions such as climate

ecotourism form of tourism that aims to minimize damage to the environment, and which helps to raise money for conservation

emission production and release of gas

endangered at risk of extinction

endemic unique to a place or region

eradicate wipe out

evict remove someone from a property with the help of the law

extinct completely died out

feral living things that have gone wild

global warming rising temperatures worldwide caused by an increase of gases in the atmosphere that trap the Sun's heat

greenhouse gas gas that stores heat in the atmosphere. Carbon dioxide and methane are examples of greenhouse gases.

greenwashing term coined by environmentalists to describe what a business or practice does when it falsely claims to be sensitive to the environment

habitat place where particular living things normally live

indigenous wildlife that is native to an area, or the first people that lived there

infrastructure range of structures, services, and facilities organized by a government for its people

International Union for Conservation of Nature (IUCN) organization that monitors biodiversity worldwide

lobby when people put pressure on politicians to try to influence them to vote in a certain way

mass extinction major extinction event in which a great many species die out at one time

native plants, animals, and other living things that are naturally found in a habitat

polyp (coral) anemone-like animal that builds the structure that becomes coral reefs

quota allotted share

renewable will not get used up

subsistence hunting hunting to provide just enough food and other products to be able to survive on

sustainable managing natural resources to meet present human needs while preserving the environment and its resources

wildlife corridor strip of land linking two areas of habitat

FIND OUT MORE

Books

Caring for Habitats, Jen Green (Wayland, 2010)

Conservation, Ian Rohr (A & C Black, 2007)

Endangered Species, Malcolm Penny (Hodder Wayland, 2001)

Endangered Species (Issues), Craig Donnellan (Independence Educational Publishers, 2010)

Endangered Wildlife, Jen Green (Green Gate, 2010)

National Parks and Conservation Areas, Jen Green (Wayland, 2009)

Protecting the Planet, Pamela Dell (Compass Point Books, 2010)

Sustainability and Environment (Issues), (Independence Educational Publishers, 2008)

Sustaining Our Natural Resources, Jen Green (Heinemann Library, 2011)

Websites

Websites about environmental protection

US Environmental Protection Agency: **www.epa.gov**

Environment Agency UK: **www.environment-agency.gov.uk**

Department for Environment, UK: **www.defra.gov.uk**

Environment Protection Authority, Australia: **www.environment.gov.au**

The Young People's Trust for the Environment: a charity which aims to encourage young people's understanding of the environment and the need for sustainability: **www.ypte.org.uk**

International Union for Conservation of Nature (IUCN): **www.iucn.org**

IUCN Red List: **www.iucn.org/about/work/programmes/species/red_list**

Marine Stewardship Council: **www.msc.org**

The Nature Conservancy: **www.nature.org**

National Parks authorities

Australia: **www.cultureandrecreation.gov.au**

European Parks Federation: **www.europarc.org/home**

New Zealand: **www.doc.govt.nz**

United Kingdom: **www.nationalparks.gov.uk**

US National Park Service: **www.nps.gov**

Environmental organizations
Friends of the Earth: **www.foe.co.uk**
Greenpeace: **www.greenpeace.org**
Sierra Club, USA: **www.sierraclub.org**
Wildlife Conservation Society (WCS): **www.wcs.org**
World Wide Fund for Nature (WWF): **www.worldwildlife.org**

Websites about deforestation
Rainforests: **rainforests.mongabay.com**
Rainforest Action Network, an environmental group which campaigns
to protect rainforests worldwide: **ran.org**
www.worldwildlife.org/what/wherewework/amazon/index.html

Topics to investigate
Find out more about sustainable development.
Global Footprint Network: **www.footprintnetwork.org**
Sustainable Development UK: **www.defra.gov.uk/sustainable/government**

Find out more about the Convention on Biological Diversity.
www.cbd.int

Find out more about the work of the IUCN and the Red List.
www.iucn.org/about/work/programmes/species/red_list

Find out more about the Red List – too big to be published in book form,
but it is available online.
www.iucnredlist.org

INDEX

Amboseli National Park 37
Antarctica 54–55

biodiversity 4, 5, 10, 12, 28, 37, 38, 39, 42, 51, 56
biomes 10
biosecurity 24, 25, 43
by-catch 48

captive breeding 40–41, 43
climate change 7, 14, 34, 52–54
coral reefs 16–17

deep ecology 8, 9, 44
deforestation 6, 12, 13, 17, 38, 39, 42, 46

ecosystems 4, 5, 10, 14, 17, 24, 39, 41, 48, 50, 53
ecotourism 34–35, 39, 47
endangered wildlife 7, 18, 19, 20, 21, 22–23, 27, 40, 43, 46, 52
endemic species 26, 38, 42
English Lake District 30
environmentalism 4, 6–9, 56–57
extinctions 4, 8, 18, 20, 22, 24, 27, 38, 44, 50, 52, 56

farming 10, 12, 17, 24, 26, 27, 36, 38, 42, 53
fish stocks 48–49, 55
food chains 14, 16, 48
"fortress conservation" 28
fur trade 19, 23, 46

genetic monitoring 40
global warming 14, 17, 21, 52, 53, 55
gorillas 35
Great Barrier Reef 17
green movement see environmentalism
green political parties 6
greenhouse gases 34, 53

Greenpeace 12, 13, 15, 19, 20
greenwashing 34

habitat conservation and restoration 39, 44, 50
habitat loss 10, 12, 16, 32, 38, 39, 42, 46, 53
Hawaiian Islands 42–43
hunting 18, 39, 43, 44–45, 46, 47

indigenous peoples 21, 36–37, 50
international agreements 7, 15, 19, 20, 23, 47, 49
International Union for Conservation of Nature (IUCN) 4, 7, 22–23, 37, 50
introduced (invasive) species 24–27, 39, 42

Kinder Scout Trespass 29

local communities 10, 31, 34, 39, 40, 43, 49, 51

Maasai 36–37
Madagascar 38–39
marine reserves 17, 55
Muir, John 6, 8, 32

Naess, Arne 8, 9
national parks and reserves 6, 10–11, 13, 28–33, 35, 36, 37, 43, 44, 47, 50, 51, 57
natural resources 8, 9, 51, 55

oceans 14, 15, 16–17, 20–21, 48–49, 53, 55
overfishing 16, 21, 48–49, 55
ozone layer 55

pollution 4, 6, 14–15, 17, 21, 30, 32, 34, 47, 52, 55
population growth 10, 39, 50, 51, 57

rainforests 12–13
recreation and tourism 11, 16, 28–35, 36, 37, 39, 42, 47, 55
recycling 7, 15, 34
Red List 22, 23
renewable technologies 34, 53
river dolphins 23

sea levels, rising 14, 53
sponsorship programmes 41
sustainability 7, 8, 39, 51, 57

tigers 46–47

waste disposal 14, 15, 31
whaling 20–21
wilderness areas 28, 31, 32
wildlife trade 18–19, 23, 35, 39, 47

Yellowstone National Park 10, 11
Yosemite National Park 32–33